S0-AFM-615

SOCIAL
ROLES AND
STEREOTYPES

WOMEN
IN THE
WORLD™

SOCIAL
ROLES AND
STEREOTYPES

ZOE LOWERY AND J. ELIZABETH MILLS

Rosen
YA™

Published in 2018 by The Rosen Publishing Group, Inc.
29 East 21st Street, New York, NY 10010

Copyright © 2018 by The Rosen Publishing Group, Inc.

First Edition

Library of Congress Cataloging-in-Publication Data

Names: Lowery, Zoe, author. | Mills, J. Elizabeth, author.
Title: Social roles and stereotypes / Zoe Lowery and J. Elizabeth Mills.
Description: New York : Rosen Publishing, 2018. | Series:
Women in the world | Includes bibliographical references and index.
Identifiers: ISBN 9781508174417 (library bound)
Subjects: LCSH: Self-perception in women—Juvenile literature. | Social perception—Juvenile literature. | Body image in women—Juvenile literature. | Stereotypes (Social psychology)—Juvenile literature.
Classification: LCC BF697.5 L68 2018 | DDC 305.235'2—dc23

Manufactured in China

CONTENTS

eminism is defined as a belief in the social, political, and economic equality of the sexes. It also refers to the movement behind this belief. Sadly, the word has often been reviled and twisted by some in the media to suggest that all feminists hate men and want to be single and childless. In reality, though, feminism is a means by which women can exercise control over their own bodies and lives.

The feminist movement seeks to make women's lives better through equality and promoting self-respect and self-confidence. Its supporters have moved forward from marches fighting for the right to vote, on to the often caricatured "bra burning" movement against the housewife stereotype of the 1950s, and now to an online community connected through blogs and social media groups. Instead of telling women what they should be doing, feminism asks women to be mindful of the choices they make, the actions they perform, and the behaviors they model. The ultimate goal is that women should be able to enjoy the freedoms passed down from previous generations and fight the new battles that come along.

In spite of this movement for women's equality and self-respect, modern technology surrounds girls and young women with media that presents itself as all-knowing about every aspect of their lives. According to DoSomething.org, a whopping 91 percent of women report being dissatisfied with their bodies and end up dieting in hopes of attaining their ideal type of body. For most, this hope is in vain, however, because a scant 5 percent of women actually have the "ideal" kind of body touted by the media. Tweens and teens are the focus of marketing and advertising companies that know full well how much buying power these girls have.

It's more common than ever to see depictions of adolescent girls in circumstances that are much too mature for their ages on the internet as well as on television. High-heeled shoes, tight, and/or low-slung jeans, tight, low-cut shirts, and elaborate makeup are lauded as style essentials for girls of ever-younger ages. And everywhere they look, girls and women are portrayed with perfect bodies and complexions. Real women and girls may suffer as a result if they don't feel like the person looking back at them from the mirror measures up.

There's only one person who can put an end to these malicious messages, keep up your self-esteem and revel in the amazing feats of your body: you

Bodies of every shape and size are unique and amazing. It's important to love your body and focus on what you can achieve with what you've got.

That's true whether you want to run marathons, dance, or enjoy any of the many activities that were banned for girls as recently as a century ago. A real revolution could occur for women and girls if they simply have the confidence to alter those burdensome centuries-old stereotypes and beliefs.

CHAPTER 1

DEFINING GENDER

Starting with headbands covered with bright pink bows and flowers for baby girls and on up to short, fitted dresses and tops for teens, society's established gender expectancies are embedded in women from birth. More often than not, women and girls are told how they should and should not behave, dress, style their hair and makeup, and even live. Usually, if an item is pink or purple, glittery and glossy, it is intended for girls. And girls often want it. What are the origins of this phenomenon? When young women are already conditioned to think, act, and speak according to gender roles? More importantly, how do females of

Gender expectations seem to begin at birth, starting with pink headbands and big flowery bows for baby girls, and continue from there.

any age free themselves from such expectations and discover their own opinions? And from there, how can they be heard over the media din and declare their opinions—positive and negative—across the globe?

"Gender" refers to the behavioral, cultural, or psychological traits that are usually associated with one sex, males or females. These roles are learned from a very young age, as children watch and listen to those around them, what adults say, and how they act.

As a child's perspective widens to include mass media, he or she watches television or browses the internet and sees characters in cartoons, shows, and commercials, as well as on websites, behave in certain ways according to their gender. Often, girls see female characters primp and preen, gossip, and fight over boys. Boys watch males wrestle and compete with one another. These moments provide a lifetime of internalized lessons on what it means to be a girl or a boy.

EVERYTHING NICE

People frequently make assumptions based on gender. They assume all girls are sweet, nice, quiet, obedient, good in school, and dreaming of their weddings. Boys are boisterous and mischievous, physical, competitive, and dreaming of becoming a pro athlete or an astronaut. Stereotypes begin as preconceived ideas about a group, assigning to them certain characteristics without regard for individuality. Society has developed and honed its gender stereotypes, its rules about females and males, and how they should act toward each other. Women may be urged to be coy and flirtatious around men they consider to be potential mates. Men may be pressed to act macho and strong and show off around women they find attractive.

In school and the workplace, females are frequently expected to go along with the group— to not make waves, to perform but not protest. If a woman speaks up, she's often labeled a troublemaker. When a male counterpart behaves the same way, however, he's just ambitious and goal oriented, natural aspirations for a man. Consider the high-profile case of Hillary Rodham Clinton. During the 2008 and 2016 presidential campaigns, Democratic candidate Hillary Rodham Clinton was often portrayed as tough and calculating, with a cold and unfeeling demeanor, and "screaming" and "shrill," despite her favorability among female voters. Her opponent for the Democratic nomination, Bernie Sanders, however, was perceived differently: "When Bernie yells, it shows his dedication to the cause," explains Jay Newton-Small in *The Washington Post.* "When [Clinton] yells, it's interpreted in a very different way: She's yelling at you." Clinton's political savvy, leadership, and intelligence—important qualities

When Hillary Clinton ran for president, she was described as loud and jarring, even though she was showing as much enthusiasm and passion for her country as her opponents.

for a presidential candidate—were considered too masculine by many media sources, as were her pant suit outfits.

There are instances in which these stereotypes are turned upside down, such as in the movie *Shrek*, in which the princess lives happily ever after…as an opinionated ogre, not a quiet princess beauty. But these examples may not be pervasive or convincing enough to overshadow the more traditional roles girls see in the media. Girls often encounter messages to speak less, eat less, and be seen less often, as evidenced by ads that show only parts of women or women covering their mouths—their desires are quenched by their invisibility. An advertisement for Exclamation perfume features the slogan "Make a statement without saying a word," suggesting the stereotype that girls don't need to express their thoughts when they can just look and smell nice to please others.

Society frequently presents modern girls with an unattainable and impossible standard of beauty and perfection. Beauty has become a willowy, waif-like, scantily clad shadow of a woman who never smiles, a doll on which clothes, makeup, and stereotypes can be hung and displayed. Together with these toxic messages, society highlights women's flaws. The media may offer solutions, effective or not, but the flaws remain and forever change women's self-perception.

BEAUTY'S BURDEN

Ironically, modern girls and women have much more opportunity than women did even fifty years ago. They enjoy reproductive freedoms in this post–*Roe v. Wade* world, power under the Equal Pay Act, and possibilities to advance and hold high offices in major companies. Nevertheless, pressures continue and worsen: women may now feel that with the option to be anything they want, they must do everything and be perfect at it. But society often won't let them be perfect. If women strive to excel at their jobs, they may be considered too career minded and not focused enough on the home. Achievers are deemed too smart; failure means they're not smart enough. It can seem like an unending, relentless onslaught of failure and unattainable perfection. Yet women are told that if they can just reach those bars society has set for them, they'll be happy. If women can lose weight and perfect their bodies, they'll be happier. Women rarely stop to consider how they're portrayed in the media or why the media seem so determined to make them feel inferior and unfinished.

Some forms of media are pure propaganda, fueled by advertising dollars, with a mission to sell something—whether it's the latest antiaging product, a fresh, fitted fashion trend, or a new diet or workout plan. The message suggests that the media know better than we do how we should live our lives. According to PRWeb, a 2013 survey by One Poll questioned two thousand women between the ages of eighteen and sixty-five. Of women ages eighteen to twenty-four 15 percent believed that the media portrayed realistic images of what models looked like in real life. Of all those polled, 33 percent felt like they had an ideal body image that would not be possible to attain. *People*

Too many people feel that the images of actors and models they see on television, in the movies, and on the internet are examples of realistic and attainable body types.

magazine conducted a poll in 2000 in which 80 percent of women interviewed felt that the way women are depicted in the media makes them feel insecure about themselves; 93 percent have tried, through diets and surgery, to look like the women they see in the media. But what these women often do not see is what the media does not show. They may not see these "perfect" women's personalities, their desires, their fears, or any of the things that make them human. Instead they may see only their outsides, a one-sided view of womanhood and humanity. They often focus on that outer shell because they're told that is important. So women can become blind to society's continued denigration of women.

In the media sources that women turn to for advice and support through their journey to perfection, women athletes are not as celebrated or given equal air time as male athletes. Women in politics are praised or criticized for their clothing choices rather than their stance on crucial issues.

A Global Media Monitoring Project (GMMP) study in 2015 reported, "Only 31% of stories on politics and 39% of economic news are reported by women." In the study, women comprised 23 percent (down from 28 percent in 2005) of those reporting "soft" news (typically art and fashion), but only reporting on 16 percent of the "hard" stories about politics and government (slightly increased from 14 percent in 2005). Furthermore, "29% of news subjects in stories reported by female journalists are women compared to 26% by male reporters. This continues a pattern first observed in 2000 when the percentages were 24% and 18% respectively." And in general, "women make up only 24% of the persons heard, read about or seen in newspaper, television and radio news," which was unchanged from 2010.

CHAPTER 2

GOOD-BYE, CHILDHOOD

Today, many dolls little girls play with are no longer wide eyed and innocent. Instead they sport ostensibly sexy, fashionable clothes and hairstyles and wear heavy makeup, as is the case with the Bratz dolls, which are a product created by MGA Entertainment. The original glitzy dolls Cloe, Jada, Sasha, and Yasmin were joined by Raya in 2015. They are easy to spot, with oversized heads balanced atop stick-thin bodies. Rather than dolls from the past, which promoted mothering and nurturing through role play, dolls like Bratz make physical attractiveness the focus of the game.

This franchise has extended beyond the toy aisle into a movie, a TV series, a reality TV show, video games,

This quartet of actresses play the original Bratz characters in *Bratz: The Movie*. Bratz dolls feature heavy makeup and sexy clothes, which may not be positive images for young girls.

a Bratz YouTube channel, featuring stop-motion animation and music albums, and a website where girls can create their own Bratz character and other girls can comment on the character's style. There is even a lingerie set for young girls, with a padded bra and bikini underpants, sized for preschoolers.

The brand does make an effort to characterize the Bratz as creative, making statements on the Bratz website, such as "The Bratz believe in thinking for themselves, creating the things they dream of, and making every day an absolute adventure." However, these dolls seem to embody our society's expectations and pressures for today's young girls—perceived perfection through constant attention to appearance and fashion, a demand rather at odds with girls who are changing both psychologically and physiologically at an ever younger age. But consumers are speaking out. In 2008, Scholastic Inc., a children's book publisher, decided to stop carrying books based on the Bratz characters in its book clubs and at book fairs after repeated urging by parents' groups.

SO LONG, CHILDHOOD

Many girls develop physically much earlier than even just a generation ago, sometimes having their first menstrual period before age ten. They grow breasts and hips earlier in life and sometimes face attention, usually unwanted, from the opposite sex. As these girls become women, they have not yet caught up emotionally to process the implications and responsibilities involved in the change.

Not so long ago, many girls learned about puberty at home, where they could ask questions and usually receive useful, honest information, thereby learning to value themselves and their inner qualities. Now with parents working long hours and often unavailable or unwilling to tackle such sticky topics, girls frequently turn to their friends and the media for answers to questions too sophisticated and embarrassing to bring up at home.

The messages they hear, see, and read can point toward the unending, unrelenting race to achieve perfection. At a time when changing bodies means fluctuating weight, erratic skin conditions, and a myriad of other uncertainties, some girls enter that race trying to gain perfection. They begin to place a high importance on their appearance, their clothes, and how "hot" they are—which apparently can be decided only by others. In grade school, many of these girls were confident and strong, but as they move into middle school, many experience anxiety and depression, and their self-esteem can fall apart, making them susceptible to risky behaviors, including unprotected sex, eating disorders, and substance abuse. What did these girls want to become before they were told to be sexy and beautiful and perfect?

ON SCREEN

Gender divisions have become more prevalent across television, movies, video games, and the internet. Teens can watch hundreds of hours of television a year, complete with thousands of commercials, many of which depict sexualized content. Many shows teens watch contain graphic material, both sexual and violent, which desensitizes them to the content. Tween girls—girls between the ages of eight and fourteen—are watching, too, and they can become numb, even if they don't understand what they're watching.

According to the Media Smarts website, a 2011 study showed that television was the means by which most young people were exposed to sexual content. About 75 percent of the children polled said that they had seen sexual content on television. Even shows that are geared toward young people, such as *Gossip Girl*, *Glee*, *Degrassi*, and *Hannah Montana* feature sex and sexuality in their plots.

According to author Daniel Weiss, a 2005 survey conducted by the Kaiser Family Foundation found that of the top twenty shows teens watched, 70 percent included sexual content in some form and about 45 percent contained sexual behavior. Furthermore, writes Tim Winters in a Parents Television Council report, all network series shown on broadcast television are rated suitable for ages fourteen or younger, "even those with graphic beheadings, bodies cut in half, fungi-infested corpses, brutal torture and, unbelievably, programs that use the sexual exploitation of children and rape as humor." According to the American Academy of Pediatrics, children younger than eight cannot discern whether something is make-believe or real, and they can learn that violence is a useful way to solve problems.

It's a similar situation with movies. The Motion Picture Association of America (MPAA) began rating movies back in 1968, and late in the 1990s they began to explain each one. Between 1990 and 2013, sex or violence was included in five out of every ten movies rated PG or higher, while cursing occurred in eight out of ten, states Randy Olsen. This could imply that the MPAA has lowered its standards for movie ratings, allowing more compromising content to be shown in movies of the same rating than before. One possible solution might be a universal rating system that would enable parents to better understand and control the content their children see.

FILM RATINGS EXPLAINED

The Motion Picture Association of America (MPAA) began rating movies back in 1968, and in the late 1990s they included specific reasons for each of their ratings: "sexual content," "drug use," "violence," and "strong language." Each MPAA rating is displayed in a box, which describes the following, according to filmratings.com:

"**RATING**   Every film is assigned a rating (G, PG, PG–13, R, or NC–17) that indicates its level of content so parents may decide whether the movie is suitable for their children.

RATING DEFINITION This   language   provides a more detailed explanation to parents of what the specific rating means.

RATING DESCRIPTORS This language is unique to each film to convey the elements that caused it to receive its rating."

The four MPAA ratings are as follows:

Rating	Description	Explanation
G	General admission	Suitable for viewers of all ages.
PG	Parental guidance suggested	Parents may object to some material for their young children.

PG-13	Parents strongly cautioned	Parents use caution; some material might not be appropriate for children younger than 13.
R	Restricted	Under 17 requires accompanying parent or adult guardian.
NC-17	No one 17 and under admitted	

For example, the Film Ratings website tweeted about the movie *Suicide Squad*: "@SuicideSquadWB is rated PG-13 for sequences of violence & action throughout, disturbing behavior, suggestive content & language." The ratings box always has a section that explains what, if anything, might be objectionable. Movies don't have to be rated, although most filmmakers choose to do so.

The video game industry is tremendously successful, bringing in more money in sales than movies and toys. And like television, video games can influence how children view themselves and each other. Recent studies showed that many popular video games perpetuated negative stereotypes of females by portraying women with unrealistic body

Beyoncé might be a positive role model as a strong and independent woman, but her lyrics and videos might be far too mature and sexual for her younger fans.

images and engaging in seductive behavior. Many concerned activists and citizens claim misogynistic portrayals persist or have gotten worse in 2016.

There has been a push to expand beyond the mostly male audience and develop games for girls, especially young girls. Some video and computer games have cross-merchandising in movies and TV shows, as well as dolls and other products. Others may use traditional themes for girls—games that focus on appearance, fashion, and acting older, thereby perpetuating a stereotype as well as reinforcing the messages girls already hear.

MAKING MUSIC

Beyoncé, Britney Spears, and Miley Cyrus have been superstars and role models to their young female fans. But these stars' videos and lyrics often paint a darker picture. Sexually provocative movements

Fashion and style advertisements sometimes depict young girls in adult poses and clothing, presenting an image that is well beyond their years.

and outfits complement songs that can feature violence and sexual behavior. And though the content of these songs might be aimed at teenagers, younger children seem to be listening as well. Many girls want to dress, sing, dance, and be as popular as these rock stars. The more they see and hear and mimic, the more sexualized they can become. In the case of Britney Spears, her first fans were quite young, and as they grew, she grew, becoming edgier and racier and singing harder songs.

STYLE

Everyday clothing has evolved, with t-shirts featuring racy slogans and shorts with phrases and images on the back. Our society has become so accustomed to dressing girls this way that it seems almost old-fashioned to call attention to it, and yet the message behind such fashion is clear—call attention to a girl's appearance and sexiness.

Fashion advertisements are sexualized, too, placing children in adultlike poses, mimicking sophisticated behavior. Sometimes the product being sold isn't even meant for children.

ABERCROMBIE FASHION

Abercrombie & Fitch, a clothing retailer known for its risqué clothing and messages, has frequently been involved in controversies. Abercrombie & Fitch targets eighteen- to twenty-two-year-olds; Abercrombie Kids targets seven- to fourteen-year-olds; Hollister Co. targets fourteen- to eighteen-year-olds; and a newer store called Gilly Hicks Sydney features underwear and bras, aimed at teens and young adults.

In 2002, several consumer advocacy groups filed complaints with the company regarding its sale of thongs featuring sayings such as "eye candy" and "wink wink" on the front. Outraged that such racy underwear would be made available to young girls, these groups successfully convinced Abercrombie & Fitch to cease selling the items.

Trick or treat! Although Halloween costumes have always teetered on inappropriate, whether they depict a violent slasher character or a racy nurse, the world of kid costumes has reached a new level of sex appeal and gender division. Girls can choose from outfits that seem like they should be for an adult, with fishnet stockings for a firefighter costume, and a sexy maid costume. And the options are not the same for girls and boys. While boys can be all kinds of professions, including a doctor, a gory science fiction character, and superhero, girls must often make do with several variations of cheerleader and entertainer. This does little to inspire girls' imaginations or self-esteem.

MENTAL AND PHYSICAL SIDE EFFECTS

With so much attention to appearance and attractiveness, it's no wonder that there are often serious consequences for little girls as they pass into puberty and enter the spotlight. A report released by the American Psychological Association Task Force on the Sexualization of Girls states that girls learn to treat themselves as sexual objects after exposure to so much sexualized imagery and behavior in pop culture. And such objectification can cause low self-esteem and self-hatred, depression, and anxiety, all of which can lead to eating disorders and self-mutilation.

Many studies agree: modern teens are up against astonishing coercion to be flawless in all ways—how they look, what they achieve in school, and how sexy they appear—all the while appearing as though it were effortless. But such stress will likely cause a collapse at some point. In fact, studies reveal that girls are much more liable to experience depression and consider suicide than are boys.

PICTURE PERFECT: PHYSICAL PERCEPTION

The fashion world centers around flashy shows featuring lean, serious women strutting in the newest styles. Models are galleries in the flesh, their thin bodies draped with art. Then their images are displayed on flashy magazine covers designed to attract and convince consumers that they need to look this way.

Vibrant colors and deceptive headlines advertise the latest diet or promote the newest weight-loss pill. The game is that you must think you won't be happy until you've read the latest breathless exposé and bought the products magazines' advertisers have paid to display between stories about how to improve your skin

The media's depiction of the "perfect" woman is long and lean, but most of the images they present have been highly edited and look quite different from the real-life model.

and how to snag the hottest partner. Happiness lies within, the magazines seem to say, and that happiness is attained through perfection. A perfect body—long and lean—is the media's ideal look for all women, regardless of age, size, shape, or race. But this "ideal" is only an illusion, meticulously crafted using special lenses, filters, lighting, and computer technology, preying upon the willingness of many women to do anything to attain perfection.

MIRROR, MIRROR

Prior to getting their first period, most girls experience a small weight gain. Their bodies need that extra weight to start menstruation. This process is common and normal, and most girls lose the extra weight as their bodies progress through puberty. However, at this age girls are often bombarded with skewed ideas of beauty and perfection. Everywhere, they see images of thin women in magazines, thin women in commercials, thin women on TV shows, thin women on the internet. But where do they see girls who look like them, who are experiencing all of the awkwardness of puberty?

Early on, many girls have learned to view their bodies as objects to be changed, corrected, modified, and controlled through money, diets, and cosmetics. Teen girls may pore through magazines or watch commercials for tips and tricks on how to perfect themselves. Meanwhile, many magazines try to convince girls that there's already something wrong with them before they've become women. These relentless blows to self-esteem and continuous pressures to live up to unrealistic ideals can give girls a damaged sense of self-worth. They may no longer believe in themselves and lose their confidence in their own abilities and strengths. Instead, they rely on external sources, such as friends, family, and media-fueled "role models" to approve their external qualities. According to author Erica Laurén Sanders, a study of fifth-grade boys and girls revealed that after watching a music video featuring pop star Britney Spears or a sample of the TV show *Friends*, they generally felt unhappy with their appearances. She cites an earlier study that showed that adolescents who spent more time watching TV shows and music videos were also more dissatisfied with their own bodies and had an increased desire to be thin.

When girls feel they can't ever live up to the expectations set for them by their family and friends, they can begin to feel depressed, anxious, and out of control. Without good self-esteem and a healthy body image, they may turn to their own bodies to regain a sense of control and success. If they can just lose another pound, if they can make it through a day without eating, then they're a success. What's worse, as their appearances starts to change, and people take

Some girls feel depressed and anxious if they are not living up to people's expectations. They may try to get a sense of control by changing their bodies.

notice, sufferers of eating disorders may feel even better about their efforts because now they're being noticed for something they're doing on their own, something they can control, something at which they succeed. And everywhere they turn, the media seems to buoy them in their quest for elusive perfection. Although the media is not solely responsible for causing eating disorders, our society has become obsessed with appearance, often teaching young girls to place an undue importance on how they look.

The National Eating Disorders Association has found that almost half a million teenagers suffer from eating disorders, which can be serious, or even fatal, for sufferers.

DESTRUCTIVE DIETS: EATING DISORDERS

The National Eating Disorders Association reports that about twenty million American women suffered from an eating disorder sometime during their lives, and half a million teenagers face the same struggle. Young women between the ages of fifteen and twenty-four are twelve times more likely to die from anorexia than all other causes of death. An eating disorder is an incredibly serious, potentially life-threatening mental illness in which the sufferer has extreme emotions and behaviors with respect to her weight and food intake. Untreated eating disorders can lead to death. Three main eating disorders are recognized by psychiatrists: anorexia nervosa, bulimia nervosa, and binge-eating disorder. A fourth category, eating disorder not otherwise specified (or EDNOS), includes sufferers whose symptoms are either mild forms of one of the three main disorders or combinations of them.

ANOREXIA NERVOSA

Anorexia nervosa is characterized by self-imposed starvation and extreme weight loss. Symptoms include an alarmingly low body weight, often 15 percent below healthy levels; an intense fear of gaining weight or being fat; a distorted body image; and amenorrhea— the absence of menstrual periods during a woman's reproductive years. Anorexics are usually cold—because of their low body weight—and highly fatigued, and they can suffer from a host of medical side effects of their disordered behavior, including:

- Stomach pain
- Heartburn
- Constipation
- Low blood pressure
- Dizziness
- Hair loss

They may also develop fine hairs all over their body, which is the body's attempt to keep warm. Anorexia has one of the highest mortality rates of all psychiatric disorders.

BULIMIA NERVOSA

Bulimia nervosa is characterized by a hidden cycle of extreme food consumption—called binge eating—followed by purging, in which the consumed food is eliminated through self-induced vomiting, ingesting laxatives, or excessive exercise. Bulimics may diet frequently and then binge eat out of an intense hunger from the diets. They often feel out of control before and during a binge, and the purge seems to restore that false sense of security and calm. Bulimics can suffer from many of the same medical problems as anorexics, with the added effects of:

- Tooth decay
- Digestive problems
- Potassium deficiency
- Difficulty sleeping

Bulimics may feel helpless, depressed, and anxious.

BINGE-EATING DISORDER

Binge-eating disorder is similar to bulimia nervosa in terms of the bingeing periods, but without the follow-up purging. As a result, the patient sometimes becomes overweight or possibly even obese. A woman who binge eats may occasionally or even regularly fast or diet, but there is a persistent feeling of shame, guilt, and self-hatred following a binge session.

People who suffer from eating disorders are usually malnourished, and they may lack the necessary vitamins and minerals for a healthy body. Binge eaters may develop diabetes or other conditions that can lead them to have a heart attack or stroke. They may even rupture their stomachs. Dehydration, kidney problems, stomach damage, joint problems, and osteoporosis are also possible problems associated with eating disorders.

CAUSES

Eating disorders center around food and calorie intake. They have little to do with actual food and weight and much more to do with a morbidly low self-esteem, poor body image, an innate tendency toward perfectionism,

GLOBAL ACTION

Eating disorders are a global problem, too, not a problem faced only by Caucasian, straight, cisgender, healthy young women from the middle class. Recent research indicates that eating disorders affect all genders in Western and non-Western cultures alike. According writer Natasha Hinde, in the United Kingdom 725,000 people struggle with some kind of eating disorder, and 357,261 of them suffer from a binge-eating disorder. The World Eating Disorders Action Day organization was created to address this universal issue. They endeavor to ensure that this disease is taken seriously and understood as a severe yet treatable disorder. So they presented the NINE Goals, which "are proposed as a global manifesto to be presented to and acted upon by policymakers and governments to take action on the growing epidemic of eating disorders across the globe. With the highest mortality rates of any mental illness the time for action is NOW. Effective solutions and programs should be markedly scaled up. Health systems must be structured to address early intervention with evidence-based treatment. Communities and providers must be educated on the realities of eating disorders and be able to assure access to services." Among their goals is to have June 2 officially recognized as World Eating Disorders Action Day.

and a need to control a life that feels out of control. Today, many girls mature earlier and faster than ever before, and our society often treats them as though they are older and more sophisticated than they are.

Instead of asking their mothers for information, many girls turn instead to their peers or the internet or television for role models and support and understanding. They may want to look and act like the girls and women they see on television, in the hopes of being just as successful and happy. But the models whose seemingly perfect bodies are the object of such envy are often quite normal looking or may even be emaciated in real life.

Magazine photographers frequently use special lenses, lights, and filters to soften lines, lighten or darken certain areas, and mask the common imperfections all normal bodies have. Designers use programs, such as Photoshop and Illustrator, to retouch the photos: erase skin from an arm, extend a curve of a hip, or smooth a laugh line. Most magazine photos have been altered in some way. That ideal woman in the glossy ad is too perfect to be real.

Yet this reality usually stays secret in the face of huge sales of diet pills and weight-loss programs and an endless pursuit of the sexiest body at all costs. Models' bodies once more closely resembled those of average American women. According to writer Madeline Jones, two decades ago, fashion models usually weighed about 8 percent less than most typical women. That figure has skyrocketed to 23 percent.

In fact, most modern models' bodies would be considered underweight based on body mass index (BMI), a barometer by which doctors measure a person's body fat content. A BMI of between 18.5 and 25 usually indicates a person is healthy with a normal weight. A BMI of 25 to 30 means a person is overweight.

OBESITY

Obesity is a medical condition in which the sufferer has a BMI of 30 or more, carrying around an excessive amount of weight and fat. It is a complex disease with physical, social, behavioral, and psychological factors that contribute to an unhealthy body composition.

A steadily increasing percentage of Americans are classified as either overweight or obese, and the most recent sufferers are children and teenagers. Just as extreme weight loss can lead to severe health problems, extreme weight gain can also cause health problems such as diabetes, heart disease, stroke, high blood pressure, and low self-esteem. Carrying this extra weight can damage joints and cause osteoarthritis, a degenerative disease of the joints that leads to swelling and pain. Obesity can lead to certain cancers, too. Many factors contribute to obesity, including genetics, depression, anxiety, addictions, binge-eating disorder, and others.

CONTROVERSIAL EATING DISORDER WEBSITES

More than four hundred websites calling themselves proanorexia or probulimia have sprung up in recent years, sparking a heated controversy. On one side of the debate are the webmasters, sometimes women with eating disorders themselves, who say that they are providing safe spaces for fellow anorexics and bulimics where they can be themselves and not be judged. They can share their stories, learn from other people, and perhaps decide to pursue recovery.

On the other side of the debate are the doctors, psychiatrists, and activists who are desperate to shut down these sites, believing they are "teaching" girls as young as ten how to become anorexic or bulimic. Many such sites feature "thinspiration"—photos of thin women, often celebrities—that serve as inspiration for continued starvation and feature tips to avoid detection by parents and doctors.

Creeds and manifestos try to elevate the disorders to a religious level, with Ana (short for "anorexia") and Mia (short for "bulimia") as goddesses of thin beauty. These sites often depict Ana and Mia as friends and being proana or promia as lifestyle choices, rather

(continued on the next page)

(continued from previous page)

than dangerous illnesses that require treatment. Though many such sites have been shut down, many more have been launched. People struggling with eating disorders do need safe spaces in which they can share their thoughts, feelings, and experiences. And they should never feel shamed or judged. It is important, however, that the information and advice they receive be in the best interests of their physical, mental, and emotional health. The very real dangers of these disorders should never be romanticized.

BODY BIAS

Remember, not every thin person has an eating disorder and not every overweight person has trouble controlling his or her appetite. People come in all shapes and sizes, and many different medical problems can result in weight loss or increase.

Overweight and obese people can face malicious treatment from people with no understanding of their situation. They may have trouble getting jobs and promotions because of their appearances—especially women. In an article by Maggie Mertens, Professor Rebecca Puhl explains that women experience weight discrimination at work at much lower levels of obesity than men do. Furthermore, she said, "Some research in the U.S. has found that among women, weight discrimination is comparable to rates of racial

You can't judge a body based on its size. Everyone's shape and size is different and one's health is the most important factor.

discrimination." The media often perpetuates this discrimination when overweight people are cast as the clown or the butt of jokes in sitcoms, while their thinner counterparts have successful jobs and relationships.

Although it's unhealthy to be obese, the path to a healthy body is tough to travel. Women with anorexia deprive themselves of food in hopes of having the same impossibly perfect body against which obese individuals are compared and derided. Our society needs to gauge beauty on people's intelligence and aptitude, regardless of their appearance.

MYTHS AND
FACTS

MYTH: Thin people are happier than fat people.

FACT: Happiness is not tied to weight. Some thin people are miserable with their bodies, and some heavier people are happy. Be as healthy as you can, eat good foods, get exercise, and learn to love yourself just the way you are.

MYTH: Older people don't have trouble getting work because they have so much experience.

FACT: Unfortunately, older people are faced with the issue of ageism, a type of discrimination because of their age. Instead of being sought after for their vast knowledge and experience, they are discriminated against for their old age.

MYTH: Media images of skinny, beautiful women cause eating disorders.

FACT: An eating disorder is a mental illness stemming from extremely low self-esteem and depression, but the prevalence of media images of unattainable beauty do help to perpetuate an artificial standard of beauty that puts far too much pressure on young women. This kind of pressure, when coupled with low self-esteem, can lead to detrimental behaviors, such as eating disorders.

THE REALITY OF MAKEOVER MADNESS

Modern reality television seems determined to promise a magical experience similar to the infamous Cinderella story, whose makeover is for the sole purpose of meeting a handsome prince and living happily ever after. Are you an "ugly duckling" or in need of the "makeover of a lifetime"? Shows like *The Swan* and *Extreme Makeover* depend on people's insecurities and low self-esteem to guarantee viewers and contestants. On *Extreme Makeover*, an Extreme Team, made up of doctors, plastic surgeons, makeup artists, cosmetic dentists, trainers, nutritionists, and therapists descend on the contestant, ready to wave their wands and make a fairy

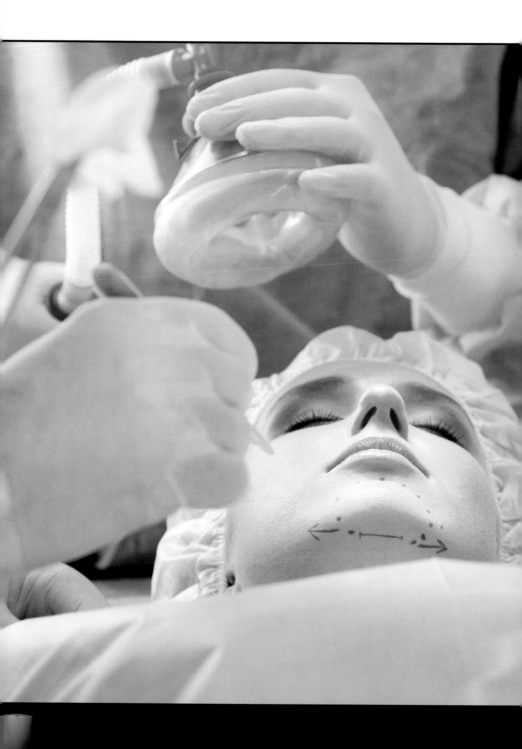

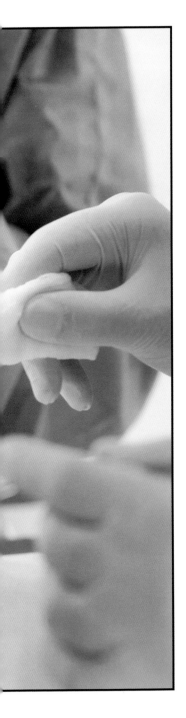

tale come true. Not only do these shows make physical attractiveness the gold standard, but they prize an artificially induced beauty that is measured against a societal definition of what is desirable. Contestants on *The Swan* (2004) believe their metamorphosis will lead to happiness and fulfillment, up until the moment when the final beauty pageant is over and the women who have worked so hard to change themselves according to arbitrary standards are sent home with only a crushed ego.

COMPARING SURGERIES

Plastic surgery is a broad field that includes both cosmetic and reconstructive disciplines. Cosmetic surgery refers to the alteration of the appearance of normal body features for aesthetic reasons. The most common body parts to undergo cosmetic surgery are breasts, ears, nose, eyes, and

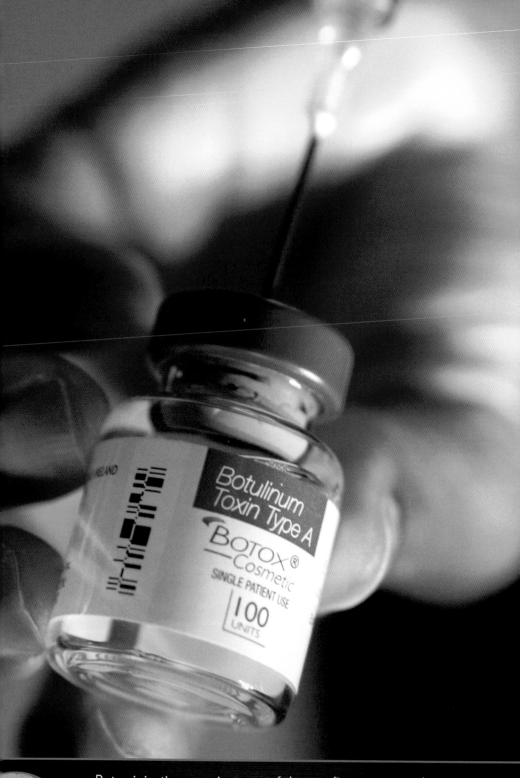

Botulinum
Toxin Type A

BOTOX®
Cosmetic

SINGLE PATIENT USE

100
UNITS

Botox injections are just one of the top five most popular
nonsurgical, or minimally invasive, cosmetic procedures

abdomen. Reconstructive surgery, however, focuses on areas of the body that are abnormal, either from congenital, or birth, defects; diseases; infections; tumors; injuries; or accidents. Both cosmetic and reconstructive surgery claim to improve quality of life through increasing self-esteem and self-confidence.

STATISTICS

According to the American Society of Plastic Surgeons, nearly sixteen million cosmetic surgery procedures were performed in 2015, with breast augmentation, liposuction, nose reshaping, eyelid surgery, and tummy tuck as the top five. That same year, Americans spent $13.3 billion on cosmetic procedures, an increase of 4 percent. Among nonsurgical, or minimally invasive, procedures, the top five in 2015 were Botox injections, soft tissue fillers, chemical peels, laser hair removal, and microdermabrasion.

THE MOST POPULAR PROCEDURES

Also known as augmentation mammaplasty, breast augmentation uses implants to increase breast size or restore breasts to their original size following significant weight loss or pregnancy. Breast asymmetry, in which a woman's breasts are not the same, is common among women but can result in low self-esteem. The asymmetry can be fixed through lifts, augmentations, or reductions. Two kinds of implants can be used: silicone, which

THE SERIOUS SIDE OF SUN-KISSED SKIN

Other aspects of one's physical appearance can be altered through methods that are less dramatic than plastic surgery, though they have their own risks and concerns as well. Tanning is a lucrative industry. The images on roadside billboards of perfectly bronzed women lying on the beach look appealing in the middle of winter, so women seek out ways to look sun kissed all year long.

There are several ways to tan, or darken, your skin color. There is no such thing, though, as a safe tan.

The first, most obvious, way is to go out into the sunshine. Sun tanning, however, is limited to the summer months and exposes you to ultraviolet ray A (UVA), which tans your skin, and B (UVB), which burns your skin and can lead to skin cancer and premature aging.

Another method is to visit a tanning salon. About thirty million people visit tanning salons each year. These salons use UVA, so you won't burn your skin. However, studies have shown that it can cause a dangerous kind of skin cancer called malignant melanoma, which is often fatal if left untreated. In

(continued on the next page)

Getting a bronzed glow might sound safe compared to plastic surgery, but tanning is not without its risks.

(continued from previous page)

addition, the light in tanning beds is concentrated almost to the level of the sun. Studies show that monthly visits to a tanning salon can increase your risk of skin cancer by as much as 55 percent.

Despite the various dangers surrounding tanning, millions of people indulge in it, demonstrating the lengths some women will go to measure up to the beauty standards around them.

contain an elastic gel that feels much like normal breast tissue but need to be checked regularly to make sure there are no leaks; and saline, which contain sterile saltwater that can easily be absorbed by the body if a leak occurs.

Liposuction refers to the surgical removal of fat deposits, especially in the buttocks and thighs.

As people age, the skin around the eyes stretches, and the muscles that support them become weak. Fat can gather above and below the eyelids, resulting in sagging eyebrows and upper lids as well as bags under the eyes. The person may start to look older and even have trouble seeing. Eyelid surgery, or blepharoplasty, removes excess skin, muscle, and fat from the eyelids.

Also known as rhinoplasty, nose reshaping restructures the nose for cosmetic purposes or to improve function by improving breathing and reducing snoring. Surgeons can change the size of the nose, the width at its bridge, the size and position of the nostrils, and the nose profile.

The tummy tuck, also known as abdominoplasty, restores a firm, streamlined figure through the surgical removal of excess fat and skin.

Botox, short for "botulinum toxin," has been around for decades and has been used for various medical purposes, including the temporary reduction or removal of lines on the forehead, around the eyes, and in the neck. A toxin is a poison, and in the case of Botox injections, the toxin paralyzes the muscles that cause wrinkles for a short period of time, resulting in smoother skin.

DANGEROUS BEAUTY

Any kind of surgery has its risks, and cosmetic surgery can lead to all kinds of problems. TV shows often make cosmetic surgery seem easy and pain free, but that is not usually the case. Many of the procedures described previously are painful and require different recovery times. Sometimes additional procedures are needed to facilitate recovery.

There are long-term risks and failures as well. In the case of breast augmentation, silicone implants can leak, leading to arthritis-like pain, swollen joints, and lupus, a disease of inflamed skin. The toxin in Botox has been known to cause botulism, a sometimes fatal, paralyzing disease. Botox can also leak into nearby muscles, weakening them and leading to more side effects.

The anesthesia used during cosmetic surgery can cause blood clots, which can lead to heart attacks and death. Asymmetry can also occur, as well as irregularities, depending on the doctor's ability and your own body's physique.

REASONS FOR COSMETIC SURGERY

Cosmetic surgery is a lucrative business, and it is in a business's best interest to have demand for its services. The media is often ready and willing to provide. All around us are images of physical "perfection"—perfect breasts, legs, buttocks, and faces. There seems to be an expectation that a woman's body should look a certain way, whether naturally or artificially.

Media outlets often tell women to look like the celebrities who set the standard for beauty in our society. And if women are not constantly trying to improve their bodies somehow, then they are not

The cosmetic surgery industry brings in a lot of money, so it
is to the industry's benefit to have all kinds of "perfect" faces

taking care of themselves. The underlying message is that women are not already perfect the way they are. If they were, women would have no reason to spend money. Cosmetic surgery claims to offer a way to attain that perfection and, as a result, possibly gain a heightened self-esteem and a better life.

Fear is a big factor behind the quest for perfect beauty. Fear of being alone forever, rejection from others, losing or not being hired for a job because of looks, or getting old. According to a study done by the American Society of Plastic Surgeons, 13 percent of working-age women interviewed said they would consider getting a cosmetic medical procedure to enable them to feel more confident and more competitive at work.

A USC professor conducted a study that reveals that after watching reality TV shows related to plastic surgery, women are more apt to experience apprehension over their body image. Increased viewing of such shows results in heightened apprehension as well as depression. Women fixate on the idea that their bodies are imperfect and develop a less-than-healthy preoccupation over how they look.

A PRECARIOUS BALANCE: FAMILY AND CAREER

From the time they are little, girls are often encouraged to pretend they are brides getting married. As they mature, media sources reinforce these ideas. Newsstands overflow with bridal magazines with headlines glorifying sumptuous celebrity weddings. Reality TV programs such as *The Bachelorette* (2003–) offer lessons on relationships and how to meet your dream husband. And television shows such as *Bridezillas* (2004–2013) reinforced a ridiculous focus on preparing for and executing the wedding day.

All this suggests to girls of all ages that a perfect wedding day to begin a perfect marriage can happen only if one spends a tremendous amount of money. According to a survey conducted by The Knot website, the average cost of a wedding in 2015 was $32,641, up an additional $5,000 from 2010.

AFTER "I DO"

But once the wedding day is over and the sun comes up again, a new life begins, and there aren't nearly as many magazines or TV shows that prepare the newlywed for the work involved in marriage. Marriage can be a wonderful thing, providing companionship, stability, financial support, and assistance in raising children. It is often viewed as the inevitable next step for a stable, committed relationship, whether both partners want it or not. But unless roles are clearly defined from the beginning, both the husband and wife are at risk of slipping into traditional roles, leading to an unequal relationship. Starting with a couple's decision whether or not to have children to the shared responsibilities for raising kids and doing chores, the traditional split can

Television shows like *Bridezillas* suggest that a wedding day—and subsequent marriage—can be perfect only if the couple spends a lot of money on the big day

be a pervasive and powerful one. The "perfect" wife was once expected to stay home, raise the children, take care of the household, and support her husband in his career.

Many programs such as the Family Formation and Development Project and Marriage Savers—funded by conservative groups—try to convince couples that the woman's role is to raise the children and keep house, and she should welcome the role as a fulfilling responsibility. They stress that having children is the most important thing a woman can do in her life (after getting married, of course), and she should embrace it. To decide not to have children is considered just as unconventional and strange as deciding to remain single. It is as though because women can have children, they should. The same conservative groups that advocate for traditional roles in marriage also encourage procreation, but they often do not consider the needed support when the baby arrives, bringing with it piles of bills and stress.

WORKING OUTSIDE THE HOUSE

Women can face many difficult decisions when it comes to having children. But perhaps one of the hardest is whether to stay home after a baby is born or to go back to work. This decision is sometimes made for a woman whose job does not offer paid or unpaid family leave. But in the instance when she can make the decision, often there isn't the flexibility for a lengthy maternity leave or a flexible part-time work schedule that would enable some time at home.

The United States is one of a few UN countries (out of a total of 193) that do not offer paid maternity leave

If she decides to have children, a woman must decide if and

to working women. Instead the government guarantees twelve weeks of unpaid leave to women who work in companies with more than fifty employees (but they must have worked there for a full year, or 1,250 hours) under the Family and Medical Leave Act, one of two federal laws involving women and childbirth, neither of which guarantee paid leave. The other law is the Pregnancy Discrimination Act, passed in 1978, which makes it unlawful to discriminate against working women based on pregnancy or childbirth. Prior to the passage of this act, employers would force women to leave the workforce when they became pregnant or had a baby. California, Rhode Island, Washington, New Jersey, and the District of Columbia are the only US places that guarantee its residents paid family leave.

The majority of American moms work outside the home. Most women can't afford not to work. The cost of living has become so high that in 2015 almost 61 percent of households with children are two-income households. But this causes its own set of problems. First, many women are already experiencing a "wage gap" in the workplace, in which they are often paid less than a man doing the same job. Once women have children, they may experience a "mommy wage gap," in which mothers earn just 77 cents for every dollar men earn, according to Kay Hymowitz of The Daily Beast, and single mothers earn even less. Then as a mother has more kids, her salary may decrease incrementally.

Furthermore, even in 2012, according to Husuna Haq, of the *Christian Science Monitor*, mothers are 44 percent less likely to be hired than women without children who have the same qualifications, and when they are hired, they're frequently offered a much lower starting pay. Conversely, if women choose to stay home because it costs less to take care of their own children than to work and pay for child care, employers may lose trained staff that contribute to the bottom line. As a result, the employer must recruit and train new employees and lose productivity time in the process.

Great Britain passed a law in 2003 enabling parents to request flexible work from the employer through a series of discussions. Unfortunately, this law doesn't exist in the United States, but websites like momsrising.org advocate for and help implement flexible work arrangements because they benefit both the mother and the employer. If a mother is happy and feels she is managing life both at home and at work, then she is often a more satisfied and productive worker who will remain loyal to her company, resulting in better output and less money and time spent on recruiting and training.

THE COST OF CARE

For some women, the option to stay at home makes more sense, fiscally and emotionally. Child care, even average-quality child care, is costly, and high-quality child care can be prohibitively expensive. A study by the Economic Policy Institute (EPI) places the yearly cost of child care for an infant at anywhere from around $17,000 in Massachusetts, to less than $5,000 in Mississippi. Regardless of a family's income and expenses, it is often a huge financial burden. The EPI also found, "As a share of total family budgets, center-based child care for single-parent families with two children (ages 4 and 8) ranges from 11.7 percent in New Orleans to 33.7 percent in Buffalo, New York." Dozens of studies have cited the importance of quality early-childhood education for a child's future academic and social success, and yet our society does not provide a means for all children to receive this kind of care. In 2014 all but two countries as well as the United States, provided paid maternity leave.

Once a mom has made the decision to stay home, though, she begins a whole new kind of full-time job, one that is unpaid and often unappreciated. In fact, even women who work outside the home may also do the majority of the work at home and take care of the kids before and after work. Many women feel they have to become supermom—the perfect mom, the perfect wife, and the perfect career woman all at the same time. This pressure seems to be exacerbated by the media and its advertisements filled with supermoms who work, make dinner for the kids, clean the house,

COMPARING CHILD CARE ACROSS THE GLOBE

Child care is a priority for families across the globe. Belgium, France, and Italy offer free and voluntary preschool, and their enrollment is at almost 100 percent. The programs offer seven to eight hours of care per day. Scandinavian countries—Denmark, Sweden, and Finland—also offer subsidized preschool, though not for as long. Largely, the government funds all of these programs. In France, the government pays two-thirds of the cost and parents cover the rest. In Italy, employers share part of the financial burden with the government. Various European countries have not only provided paid paternity leave for many years but also encouraged it. They want to support joint parenting responsibilities from the birth of the child.

and pay the bills all single-handedly. And she does it all with a smile.

Situations in which the father stays home and cares for the children are rare, but growing. In 2014, the US Census reported 1.9 million stay-at-home dads. In addition, there is a trend toward equality in parenting,

A mother's job may not bring in a paycheck, but it certainly

in which the father takes an equal role in caring for the children and the home. Although these situations often occur at higher income levels, they signify a shift away from traditional family roles, which should help reduce stress mothers feel about returning to work.

MEASURING MOTHERHOOD

The job of motherhood requires an extraordinary ability to simultaneously juggle many responsibilities. It involves utilizing skills in project management, multitasking, and managing human resource needs. It has been reported that a full-time, stay-at-home mother would earn a salary comparable to that of an ad executive or a judge. A mother who works outside the home would earn thousands more. The study was conducted from an assessment of the earnings of people whose jobs were performed by a mother—housekeeper, day-care teacher, cook, computer operator, and janitor, just to name a few.

CHAPTER 6

EMBRACING AGING

The plastic surgery industry is not the only one to cash in on the fear of aging; the cosmetics industry produces copious shiny ads for merchandise that supposedly helps maintain youthful vibrant skin to counteract the body's natural process of aging. It's wise to protect your skin from the environment's negative effects, but the aging process cannot be stopped or reversed. Nevertheless, thanks to the combination of smart marketing and a lack of Food and Drug Administration (FDA) parameters, there are no limits to what benefit a product can declare it provides, and a high price may convince buyers that it is worth the cost. Most antiaging advertisements also feature women far too young to be concerned with wrinkles and loose skin. When did the prospect of aging become so

The cosmetics aisle is filled with creams that claim to slow the aging process, but the fact remains that aging is a natural part of everyone's life.

abhorrent that women (and sometimes men) feel like they have to do just about anything possible to put it off?

DEFINING "OLD"

At one time, sixty-five was considered old. Then, it was seventy-five. Now, people are living well into their seventies, with women expecting to live to eighty. The average life expectancy in the United States is seventy-nine years according to the World Bank. How long an individual actually lives is based on a combination of genetics, environment, and the luck of the draw. In 2016, 15 percent of the total population was older than sixty-five. The Census Bureau projects that "by 2050, the proportion of the population 65 and older (15.6 percent) will be more than double that of children under age 5 (7.2 percent)." The majority of the older population are women. The oldest country in 2016 was Japan, followed by European countries, Canada, and Puerto Rico, all making up the top twenty-five.

Humans begin aging in the womb. Cells in the body contain genetic material called DNA, which breaks down as the cells replicate. Substances called free radicals are released that do damage to the cells and other parts of the body. But the body produces countermeasures called free radical scavengers that seek out and remove free radicals. That process works for a while. Eventually, the body loses its ability to fight the free radicals. As the damage accumulates over the years, it results in diseases and changes that society attributes to aging. Human bodies operate less efficiently, processes change and stop working, skin becomes tighter and less elastic, bones and joints become brittle and are broken easily, and organs wear out.

But aging is an individual experience; for some people, the aging process does not hinder their lives dramatically and they stay in relatively good health until their death. For others, aging can cause all kinds of problems, physical and mental, and the process becomes difficult. Studies reveal that temperament may play a role in how aging occurs. If older people accept the stages of getting older and stay positive about the good things in their lives, they may experience a healthier aging process.

AN AGING EXTRA: MENOPAUSE

For women, the aging process includes an extra change—menopause. Usually during their mid-forties or early-fifties, women enter a new life phase, in which reproduction comes to an end. Menstruation ceases, and the ovaries gradually make less and less of the hormones estrogen and progesterone.

Each woman's menopause experience and symptoms will differ. Common symptoms include altered periods (they might become shorter or longer, lighter or heavier, with more or less time in between them); hot flashes and night sweats; trouble sleeping through the night, at times caused by night sweats; mood swings in which a woman can feel irritable or experience crying spells; trouble focusing or forgetfulness; hair loss or thinning hair; or facial hair growth.

Estrogen helps to build and maintain bone density throughout a woman's development. As the female body ceases to produce estrogen, women can experience bone loss, causing weak bones to break easily. This loss can lead to osteoporosis, a condition characterized by a decrease in bone mass. While there are no special treatments for menopause, menopausal hormone therapy (MRT) can sometimes help reduce the severity of some symptoms. A healthy diet and regular exercise are recommended as well. Estrogen therapy can be one method for alleviating the symptoms.

PREJUDICES AGAINST AGE

Ageism is the stereotyping of and discrimination against individuals or groups because of their age, based on a set of beliefs that justify the discrimination. The term "ageism" was first used by a gerontologist, someone who studies aging and older people, named Robert N. Butler. He invented the term to describe the prejudice he saw against senior citizens, which he felt was patterned on racism and sexism. Ageism includes prejudicial attitudes toward older people, old age, and the aging process; practicing discrimination against the aged; and institutional practices that perpetuate stereotypes about seniors. Unfortunately, ageism is still considered one of the last acceptable forms of discrimination. Society often expects its older citizens to withdraw from society—from its responsibilities and its culture—and retreat to shared communities with other older folk, where they can be protected and sequestered. The negative stereotypes around old age seem to encourage that kind of withdrawal. A culture in which a person's dignity and self-worth are caught up in his or her ability to contribute through employment certainly conveys the idea that there is no place for retired citizens.

Ageism perpetuates stereotypes that older people are inactive and don't take care of themselves. It also suggests that they're dependent, forgetful, infantile, unreliable, incompetent, asexual, cute, and grandmotherly or grandfatherly.

As with any stereotype or prejudice, ageism stems from a need to set oneself apart, to seem unlike those being mocked. Old people may scare younger people because they represent the future. Young people may realize that one day, they might be that old, they might forget things and stumble and lose their way. But not yet, they tell themselves, even those who are in the middle of their lives, not so far away from old age. They believe they are still young and still vibrant and still meant to be a part of the contributing public.

NEGATIVE SELF-IMAGE

Studies have shown that the negative effects of ageism are visible in older people's lowered self-esteem and

The objects of ageism might feel slow and useless, leading to a negative perception of themselves. Studies show that optimism can actually prolong your life, though!

behaviors. They may be able to shrug off the prejudices, or they may internalize them to such an extent that they eventually become forgetful and doddering and uncoordinated. Older people are often made to feel useless, no longer able to contribute to our fast-paced, high-tech world. The time they need to complete tasks, process new information, or cross the street can anger and frustrate the speed-concerned young, who often shout insults and prejudicial comments at them.

A study conducted by lead researcher Becca Levy, Ph.D., at Yale University's Department of Epidemiology and Public Health, concluded that older people who have positive self-perceptions of aging tended to live 7.5 years longer than those whose self-perceptions of aging were more negative. Optimism can have a greater influence even than many physiological conditions on the length of a person's life, the study found. Conversely, exposure and internalization of negative stereotypes and low self-esteem can measurably shorten a person's life.

WORKPLACE DISCRIMINATION

Ageism can be present in many aspects of a person's life, but its influence can perhaps be felt the most in the workplace. Employers may face increased health care costs as their employees age. Many older citizens looking for jobs may not have or may be unable to acquire the necessary skills to be able to perform modern, high-tech jobs. These facts can discourage many employers from hiring and retaining older employees. As of 2014, more than thirty countries had instituted various age-discrimination laws. The laws in Britain and Denmark, for example, are modeled on the European Union's Employment, Equality (age) Regulations, which call for equal treatment in the workplace regardless of religion or belief, disability, age, or sexual orientation.

In Denmark and Britain, it is illegal to discriminate on the basis of age in all aspects of recruitment, dismissal, training, and retirement prior to age sixty-five. But Denmark has one major difference from Britain: Danish employees are not automatically able to request to continue working beyond age sixty-five. British employees have been able to since 2006.

In the United States, the Age Discrimination in Employment Act makes it illegal to fire or fail to hire a person based on his or her age if the employee is older than the age of forty. But this law offers little protection in terms of training and benefits, and despite this law, employment in those older than fifty has decreased. The workplace has changed over the years since the law was passed, making it harder for older people to stay at their jobs. But some changes are happening; more claims of age discrimination are being lodged in retaliation, and states like California now require that managers take special training classes on age, race, and sex discrimination.

The bottom line is that laws can have only so much effect. Older people are often still having trouble finding work. Our society must change how it views our senior citizens, employed or retired, by accepting them as meaningful, contributing people with their own needs and demands.

DON'T BE CRUEL

Ageism can affect older women and men at home, as well. Many senior citizens who live by themselves are victims of physical, emotional, and financial abuse. They can be the victims of scams, robberies, and violence. Sometimes the attacker is a stranger looking to get some quick cash by posing as a utility worker. But more often than not, it may be a caregiver, even a relative, who instigates the violence in search of money. Stereotypes that the elderly are weak and easily confused buoy those who would do them harm, thinking seniors are easy targets. Unfortunately, few cases of elder abuse are actually reported to the police, often because the elderly have trouble facing the fact that they're vulnerable after being self-sufficient for so many years. Giving up their driving privileges to take public transportation and giving up their homes to move to retirement communities can be painful enough to an older individual who feels as though he or she should still be able to live independently.

FOREVER YOUNG

Wrinkles, gray and brittle hair, skin that sags and feels papery dry—all outward signs of a body getting older, and all things we vow to correct with the newest products in a highly profitable market. In 2005, American women spent $664 billion on products that promised antiaging miracles. Today, the amount is close to $2 billion. A few common remedies supposedly turn back the clock. The human growth hormone (HGH), an antiaging hormone injection, has been shown in some studies to stimulate muscle development, improve mental abilities, and reduce bone loss. But these effects have been demonstrated through regular exercise as well. HGH can have harmful side effects as well as being expensive. Waters also claim to stop or reverse the aging process. Glorified mineral waters have been magnetized or altered to supposedly improve hydration beyond ordinary water. Some vitamin products claim to contain antioxidants that can remove free radicals before they do cell damage. A simpler method is to eat a healthy diet that contains these vitamins.

One of the best ways to keep your body fit and healthy as you get older is to exercise. While it won't affect the aging process itself, physical exertion improves mental stamina and acuity; improves mood; reduces risks of osteoporosis, heart disease, stroke, cancer, and diabetes; and even makes the body look better. It may possibly add years to your life and improve your quality of life.

Accomplished actors like Dame Judi Dench help break the stereotype that women must be young to be leading ladies. Dench was seventy-nine when she won an Oscar.

HOLLYWOOD AGEISM

There seems to be a double standard in Hollywood when it comes to older actresses. Called Hollywood ageism, it refers to the difficulty older actresses have in finding roles as their faces and bodies age. Gone are the sexy parts, both in terms of their limelight and their demands for youthful beauty, from the résumes of Hollywood's older women. Interestingly enough, Hollywood men don't seem to suffer the same discrimination, as Sean Connery, Richard Gere, and Pierce Brosnan demonstrate, with their mature charm and stylish silver hair. The awards ceremonies are no different. Women who win in the Best Actress category are frequently younger than their Best Actor counterparts when they win their first Oscar. In 2007, Helen Mirren was the fourth-oldest actress in the history of the awards to win the Oscar for Best Actress. No lead actress between the ages of fifty and fifty-nine has ever won an Oscar. Jessica Tandy was the oldest actress to win, at eighty, and Dame Judi Dench won in 2013 at age seventy-nine. Dench was older than sixty for all seven of her Oscar nominations, so things do seem to be looking up in the vain Hollywood culture the last few years. Furthermore, there have been more leading roles for mature women in movies like *The Queen*, *The Devil Wears Prada*, and others.

1. What do I do if I know someone who has an eating disorder?

2. Why does the media continue to make and air such stereotypical commercials when they know they're bad for girls?

3. How do I know if plastic surgery is right for me?

4. How do I find out if my acne-fighting product is bad for my skin?

5. What are some ways I can help endorse better portrayals of girls in the media?

6. How can I go about fighting ageism and support the older people around me?

7. How can I advocate for government-subsidized child care?

8. What are some healthy ways I can take care of my body without damaging my body image?

9. What can I do to help promote the case for the United States putting a BMI limit on its supermodels?

10. What are some ways I can help redefine gender roles?

THE FUTURE LOOKS BRIGHT

Despite mounting challenges, society needs to figure out how to reframe the way people consider and depict women as well as their body image. The beauty business will always be just that—a business—and keeping control of that provides it with a lot of influence. But women are partially to blame for these pervasive negative clichés as long as they buy the periodicals that belittle and objectify them. Women have the power to make great changes simply by supporting organizations that uplift the women who read and buy their products. Some teen-oriented periodicals, fashion shows, and apparel dealers have already made this seemingly tiny step that will hopefully lead to many more such steps to a world that eschews this fixation on appearance.

TEENS SPEAKING OUT!

If you look carefully, you can find an unusual and powerful publication, *Teen Voices*, which, according to its website, is "changing the media landscape one byline at a time. Girl-produced news for a global audience." Started in Cambridge, Massachusetts, in 1988 by two young women, *Teen Voices* became part of the Womens eNews website in 2013. Articles tackle issues including anorexia, wearing the hijab, and feelings of unworthiness.

The editorial staff is made up of teens and adults who receive thousands of submissions from teens across the globe on all kinds of topics—politics, book reviews, arts, health, activism, and more. Its focus is on making sure teen girls are heard for what they have to say, amidst all the media chatter about how they should be. The staff works with low-income girls of color to build confidence both in themselves and in their ability to critically evaluate and write about the world around them. Workshops for the teen editors help address real-life problems such as sexual harassment, money management, and sexually transmitted diseases. *Teen Voices* wants teens to use their words, thoughts, and ideas to bring awareness and change to issues that matter to them. By teaming up with Women's eNews, *Teen Voices* now speaks with a more global, multicultural voice. They provide mentoring and writing opportunities as well as programs such as the Teen Voices Virtual Newsroom. They also have a presence on social media, including on Facebook, Twitter, and tumblr. Look for the hashtag #BeHeard.

GLOBAL CHANGE

Countries around the globe are speaking out about body image, eating disorders, and the appalling thinness rampant at high-profile fashion shows.

In April 2008, Valérie Boyer, the deputy of Marseilles, France, declared war on anorexia. She proposed a bill targeting proanorexia websites, as well as the fashion magazines and advertisers who perpetuate this dangerous standard of beauty. Penalties include a fine and possible jail time.

French fashion houses and advertisers have signed a voluntary charter, pledging to promote body diversity and healthy body image, and to refrain from using images of youth that advocate extreme thinness. The charter, which came after two supermodels died, does not set body size and weight limits.

In 2015, France also proposed a bill that required models who want to work in France to provide confirmation from their doctors that they are

The deputy of Marseilles, France, Valérie Boyer, sought to charge proanorexia websites with fines and jail time. Periodicals and advertisers were in her line of fire, too.

healthy enough to work. The same legislation requires periodicals and advertisements to label any image that has been touched up, or changed digitally to alter the appearance of the model. There are an estimated forty thousand anorexics in France, many of whom are teenagers.

In Italy, the government and representatives of Italian designers are requiring models to demonstrate that they are healthy and not suffering from an eating disorder. They have banned models who are younger than sixteen and have called for designers to commit to adding larger sizes to their collections.

In the United States, the Council of Fashion Designers of America (CFDA) organizes the huge biannual fashion week in New York. The council has put out a list of guidelines for the models to encourage them to follow healthy eating patterns. The guidelines encourage education about eating disorders and dietary issues, and they discourage models younger than sixteen from participating. But there are no weight limits for the models to follow. CFDA's position is about awareness rather than regulation.

The strongest measures have been taken in Madrid, Spain, where there have been three major initiatives to combat eating disorders and body image issues. First, in 2006, Spain banned 30 percent of the models from its fashion shows who had a BMI less than 18, meaning a minimum weight of 123 pounds (56 kilograms) for a height of 5 feet 7 inches (170 centimeters). These guidelines are in accordance with the World Health Organization's guidelines for healthy height-to-weight ratios.

Second, the Spanish government called for a standardization of women's clothing sizes. Throughout the world, women's clothing sizes differ from store to store and country to country, with some retailers artificially lowering sizes to improve women's self-

Some Spanish clothing retailers have agreed to remove their excessively thin mannequins and replace them with those that model a more reasonable body size.

esteem and encourage sales. To better understand the body sizes and shapes of its female citizens, the government used high-tech booths fitted with lasers that need only thirty seconds to take 130 measurements of a woman's body. These booths have appeared throughout Spain, and ten thousand volunteers from the ages of twelve to seventy took part in the study. The data will be passed on to clothing designers, who will redesign their clothes and sizing to match real women, not super thin models. The study found that almost 41 percent of the volunteers say they have trouble finding clothes that fit them because of inaccurate sizing.

Third, major clothing retailers in Spain have agreed to pull their rail-thin mannequins from display windows and replace them with mannequins that are at least a European size 38 (US size 8). Spain also limits the times of day when television advertisements for certain beauty products can be shown to times when young children are less likely to be watching.

Spain provides an excellent role model for those countries, including the United States, that are not doing all they can to help women have healthy body images. Going forward, hopefully the United States and other countries will take a page from their book and take steps above and beyond more realistic clothing sizes to help women of every size and every culture feel strong and beautiful inside and out.

AMENORRHEA Absence of menstrual bleeding usually in young women.

ANOREXIA NERVOSA A serious disorder in eating behavior primarily of young women in their teens and early twenties that is characterized especially by a pathological fear of weight gain leading to faulty eating patterns, malnutrition and usually excessive weight loss.

BINGE-EATING DISORDER A serious eating disorder in which unusually large amounts of food are frequently consumed.

BODY MASS INDEX (BMI) A measure of body fat based on height and weight.

BULIMIA NERVOSA A serious eating disorder characterized by a cycle of binge eating followed by compensatory purging.

CISGENDER Those who identify with their biological sex; those who don't consider themselves transgender.

CONGENITAL Existing at or dating from birth.

EATING DISORDER A compulsion to eat or avoid eating that negatively affects both one's physical and mental health.

ESTROGEN A hormone produced by both men and women.

FEMINISM A belief in the social, political, and economic equality of the sexes, as well as the

GENDER The behavioral, cultural, or psychological traits typically associated with one sex.

LAXATIVE A substance that causes elimination of the bowels.

MELANOMA A malignant skin tumor.

MENOPAUSAL HORMONE THERAPY (MRT) A course of hormones that helps alleviate symptoms of menopause.

MENOPAUSE The natural cessation of menstruation that usually occurs between the ages of forty-five and fifty-five.

OBESE Describes a person with a body mass index higher than 30.

OSTEOPOROSIS A disease that weakens bone structure and causes bones to be easily fractured and broken.

OVERWEIGHT Describes someone with a body mass index between 25 and 29.

PLASTIC SURGERY A surgical discipline that covers both cosmetic and reconstructive surgeries.

PROGESTERONE A hormone produced by women that acts with estrogen and plays a role in pregnancy.

PROPAGANDA Mainly negative information, that is usually purposely incorrect or misleading, for the purpose of highlighting a specific viewpoint or idea.

RECONSTRUCTIVE SURGERY Surgery that focuses on areas of the body that are abnormal, from congenital (birth) defects, diseases, infections, tumors, injuries, or accidents.

STEREOTYPE A preconceived idea that attributes certain characteristics (in general) to all the members of a class or set.

THINSPIRATION Images or sayings that focus on the importance of being thin, often found on proanorexia and probulimia websites.

ULTRAVIOLET Light that comes from the sun.

Feminist Majority Foundation (FMF)
1600 Wilson Boulevard, Suite 801
Arlington, VA 2209
(703) 522-2219
Website: http://www.feminist.org
The Feminist Majority Foundation is dedicated
    to women's equality, reproductive health, and
    promoting nonviolence.

Girls Incorporated
120 Wall Street, 3rd Floor
New York, NY 10005
(212) 509-2000
Email: communications@girlsinc.org
Website: http://www.girlsinc.org
Girls Incorporated is a national nonprofit youth
    organization dedicated to inspiring all girls to
    be strong, smart, and bold.

Kids Help Phone
National Office
300-439 University Avenue
Toronto, ON M5G 1Y8
Canada
(416) 586-5437
Website: http://www.kidshelpphone.ca
Kids Help Phone is Canada's only toll-free, national,
    and bilingual phone and web counseling,

referral, and information service for children and youth.

National Association of Anorexia Nervosa and Associated Disorders (ANAD)
750 East Diehl Road
Suite 127
Naperville, IL 60563
(630) 577-1333
Email: anadhelp@anad.org
Website: http://www.anad.org
ANAD is the oldest eating disorder organization in the nation, and it continues to answer thousands of hotline calls each year.

National Eating Disorders Association (NEDA)
165 West 46th Street
Suite 402
New York, NY 10036
(800) 931-2237
Email: info@NationalEatingDisorders.org
Website: http://www.nationaleatingdisorders.org
NEDA is committed to providing help and hope to those affected by eating disorders.

National Organization for Women (NOW)
1100 H Street NW, Suite 300
Washington, DC 20005

(202) 628-8669
Website: http://www.now.org
The largest organization of feminist activists in
the United States, NOW works to eliminate
discrimination and harassment; secure
abortion, birth control, and reproductive
rights for all women; end all forms of violence
against women; eradicate racism, sexism, and
homophobia; and promote equality and justice
in our society.

Office on Women's Health (OWH)
Department of Health and Human Services
200 Independence Avenue SW, Room 712E
Washington, DC 20201
(202) 690-7650
Website: https://www.womenshealth.gov
The Office on Women's Health was established in
1991 with a vision to ensure that all women
and girls are healthier and have a better sense
of well-being.

Younger Women's Task Force
American Association of University Women
(AAUW)
1310 L Street NW, Suite 1000
Washington, DC 20005
(202) 785-7700

Website: http://www.aauw.org/membership/ywtf
The Younger Women's Task Force is a nationwide diverse and inclusive grassroots movement dedicated to organizing younger women and their allies to take action on issues that matter most to them.

WEBSITES

Because of the changing nature of internet links, Rosen Publishing has developed an online list of websites related to the subject of this book. This site is updated regularly. Please use this link to access this list:

http://www.rosenlinks.com/WITW/stereotypes

Ambrose, Marylou, and Veronica Deisler. *Investigating Eating Disorders*. New York, NY: Enslow Publishers, 2011.

Anderson, Laurie Halse. *Wintergirls*. London, England: Scholastic, 2016.

Angier, Natalie. *Woman: An Intimate Geography*. New York, NY: Mariner Books, 2014.

Boston Women's Health Book Collective. *Our Bodies, Ourselves: A New Edition for a New Era*. New York, NY: Touchstone, 2014. Ebook.

Chambers, Veronica. *The Joy of Doing Things Badly: A Girl's Guide to Love, Life, and Foolish Bravery*. New York, NY: Broadway Books, 2006.

Gerdes, Louise. *The Culture of Beauty*. Detroit, MI: Greenhaven Press, 2013.

Gitlin, Marty. *Combating Discrimination Against Women in the Gamer Community*. New York, NY: Rosen Young Adult, 2017.

Jones, Viola. *Conquering Negative Body Image*. New York, NY: Rosen Young Adult, 2016.

Lew, Kristi. *I Have an Eating Disorder. Now What?* New York, NY: Rosen Young Adult, 2015.

Orr, Tamra. *Combating Body Shaming*. New York, NY: Rosen Young Adult, 2017.

Pipher, Mary. *Reviving Ophelia: Saving the Selves of Adolescent Girls*. New York, NY: Riverhead Books, 2014. Ebook.

American Society of Plastic Surgeons. Plastic Surgery. Retrieved September 12, 2016. http://www.plasticsurgery.org.

Bratz.com. About. Retrieved September 12, 2016. http://www.bratz.com/en-us/about.

Brumberg, Joan Jacob. *The Body Project: An Intimate History of American Girls.* New York, NY: Random House, 1997.

Classification and Ratings Association. "What: Guide to Ratings." Retrieved September 12, 2016. http://filmratings.com.

DoSomething.org. "11 Facts About Body Image." Retrieved September 19, 2016. https://www.dosomething.org.

Edmondstone, Michael. "Women Need Further Educating Into Extent of Digital Manipulation of Models in Mags, New Look Survey Finds." November 26, 2013. http://www.prweb.com/releases/2013/11/prweb11361783.htm.

Favor, Leslie J. *Food as Foe: Nutrition and Eating Disorders.* Tarrytown, NY: Marshall Cavendish, 2008.

Forbes.com. "How Employers Wage War on Workplace Obesity." January 11, 2008. http://www.forbes.com/2008/01/11/obesity-workplace-cdc-ent-hr-cx_kw 0110whartonobesity.html.

Global Media Monitoring Project. "Who Makes the

News?" Retrieved September 13, 2016. http://
whomakesthenews.org.

Guardian. "French MPs Back Law to Bar Media
from Promoting Anorexia." April 16, 2008.
https://www.theguardian.com/world/2008
/apr/16/france.law.

Guthrie, Doug, and Charles E. Ramirez. "Violence
Against Seniors on the Rise." *AARP Bulletin
Today*, February 17, 2009. http://bulletin.aarp
.org.

Haq, Husna. "Share of Working Moms Nearing
All-Time High, But Has It Gotten Any Easier?"
Christian Science Monitor, May 11, 2012. http://
www.csmonitor.com/USA/Society/2012/0511
/Share-of-working-moms-nearing-all-time
-high-but-has-it-gotten-any-easier.

Hinde, Natasha. "Binge Eating Disorder: Symptoms
and Treatment for the Illness Affecting More
than 350,000 In the UK." Huffington Post,
February 22, 2016. http://www.huffingtonpost
.co.uk/2016/02/22/binge-eating-disorder
-symptoms-and-treatment_n_9253726.html.

Jones, Madeline. "Plus Size Bodies, What Is Wrong
With Them Anyway?" *PLUS Model Magazine*,
January 8, 2012. http://www.plus-model-mag
.com/2012/01/plus-size-bodies-what-is
-wrong-with-them-anyway.

Knot, The. "Wedding Money: What Does the Average Wedding Cost?" Retrieved October 3, 2016. https://www.theknot.com/content/what-does-the-average-wedding-cost.

Levin, Diane E. Ph.D., and Jean Kilbourne, Ph.D. *So Sexy So Soon.* New York, NY: Ballantine Books, 2008.

Mayo Clinic. "Blepharoplasty." July 18, 2007. http://www.mayoclinic.org/tests-procedures/blepharoplasty/basics/definition/prc-20020042.

Media Smarts. "Television's Impact on Kids." Retrieved September 12, 2016. http://mediasmarts.ca/television/televisions-impact-kids.

Medline Plus. "Plastic and Cosmetic Surgery." April 1, 2016. http://www.nlm.nih.gov/medlineplus/plasticandcosmeticsurgery.html.

Mertens, Rebecca." The Workplace Problem That No One Is Talking About." Refinery 29, June 26, 2015. http://www.refinery29.com/2015/06/89803/women-weight-discrimination-at-work.

Mirror Mirror. "Who Gets Eating Disorders." Retrieved September 12, 2016. http://www.mirror-mirror.org/diversity.htm.

Milbank, Dana. "The Sexist Double Standards

Hurting Hillary Clinton." *The Washington Post*, February 16, 2016. https://www .washingtonpost.com/opinions/the -sexist-double-standards-hurting-hillary -clinton/2016/02/12/fb551e38-d195-11e5 -abc9-ea152f0b9561_story.html?utm_term =.b22760658724.

Motion Picture Association of America. "Film Ratings." Accessed September 21, 2016. http:// www.mpaa.org/film-ratings.

Nyhan, Paul. "Stay-Home Fathers Figure Out Their New Full-Time Job." *Seattle Post-Intelligencer*, April 25, 2006. http://www.seattlepi.com /lifestyle/article/Stay-home-fathers-figure -out-their-new-full-time-1201907.php.

Olson, Randy. "A Look at Sex, Drugs, Violence, and Cursing in Film Over Time Through MPAA Ratings." RandalOlson.com, January 12, 2014. http://www.randalolson.com/2014/01/12/a -look-at-sex-drugs-violence-and-cursing -in-film-over-time-through-mpaa-ratings.

Parents Television Council. "Sex, Violence, and Profanity in the Media Fact Sheet, TV Statistics." April 16, 2013. https://ecfsapi.fcc .gov/file/7022283827.pdf.

Sanders, Erica Laurén. "The Influence of Media Marketing on Adolescent Girls." Undergraduate Research Community. Retrieved September

13, 2016. http://www.kon.org/urc/v8/sanders.html.

Schpoliansky, Christophe. "No More Bare-Bone Top Models in France?" ABC News, April 10, 2008. http://abcnews.go.com/International /story?id=4618002&page=1.

Tiggemann, M., and A. S. Pickering. "Role of Television in Adolescent Women's Body Dissatisfaction and Drive for Thinness." *International Journal of Eating Disorders*, Vol. 20, pp. 199–203.

Weiss, Daniel. "Sexual Content on TV Is Increasing." Brushfires Foundation, May 8, 2013. http://www.brushfiresfoundation.org /sexual-content-on-tv-is-increasing.

Winters, Tim. "In Rating Movies and TV, An Extreme Makeover Is Needed." *New York Times*, November 21, 2013. http://www.nytimes. com/roomfordebate/2013/11/21/rating-sex -violence-and-profanity-in-movies/in-rating -movies-and-tv-an-extreme-makeover -is-needed.

World Eating Disorders Day. "Nine Goals: Taking Action Against Eating Disorders." Retrieved September 28, 2016. http://www .worldeatingdisordersday.org/nine-goals -taking-action-against-eating-disorders.

ABOUT THE AUTHOR

Zoe Lowery is an avid student of history, with a particular interest in women's roles. When she's not writing or editing, Lowery enjoys experimenting with recipes in the kitchen or riding her motorcycle over the mountains or to her local library in Colorado.

Elizabeth J. Mills is a writer who is not ashamed to love sports, action movies, the occasional romantic comedy, the color pink if it's on a ballet tutu, and hiking boots. She has published many books for kids on all kinds of topics. Mills lives in Seattle, Washington, a city where women live and laugh loudly and often.

PHOTO CREDITS